The Smart Guide to

Overcoming Anxiety

By

Carmen S. Gonzalez, MS.Ed.

Step 1 is Acknowledgement

The first step to overcoming anxiety is accepting the situation for what it is. Acknowledge that there is a problem. Does fear over-ride your decisions for wanting to improve your career? Do you struggle with keeping love in your life? If you answered yes to either question, then you have begun the healing process.

Healing begins when you acknowledge that you have a problem. Many times people are not open to change because they are embarrassed. This embarrassment causes turmoil in their entire life. Fear is the reason why people are afraid to try something new.

By picking up this book, you have acknowledged that you are on your way to success. This book will give you strategies for overcoming your fears. By extinguishing your fears or taking them away and replacing them with positive thinking, you will begin to live a fulfilling life. Overcoming your fears is 99% determination on your behalf. The other 1 % is being able to go out and try new strategies. Good luck on your journey as you read this book.

A Look into your Soul

Materials:

Mirror

Procedure:

1. Look into the mirror and stare into your eyes.

2. Tell yourself: "I love myself". "I am the most important person in my life".

"I am unstoppable me". "I am fearless".

3. Chant 3 times or until you believe it.

4. Chant these affirmations 3 times a day or as needed.

By looking into the mirror, you are reflecting positive energy. It is impossible to begin your day, without believing in your abilities. By saying I instead of you, it is implied that you accept these statements to be true.

At night before bed, always restate your chants. By going to bed with calming thoughts, all of your fears are extinguished before laying your head to rest. This can result in having a positive dream during REM sleep, the dreaming state of your sleep. Some people who suffer from anxiety often report of not having dreams, since they have been replaced with preoccupation with a fear that results in loss sleep. By clearing your mind before bedtime and replacing them with positive affirmations you are compensating for the thoughts that would have occurred without an intervention.

A look into your soul is not meant to have any other connotation besides unleashing a new and better you that was always there. It is not meant to have any other belief to it. There is nothing narcissistic about looking into the mirror and saying nice things to a very important person, you. Narcissism begins when you are preoccupied with you and always looking into the mirror, but when you are recovering from anxiety, because the anxiety is due to some loss of self-esteem, this can be a great self-esteem booster.

Get energized through exercise

Materials:

Walking shoes (sneakers)

Treadmill (optional)

Water

Procedure:

1. Put on your walking shoes

2. Enjoy nature by going out for a walk.

3. Be attentive of the nature around you.

4. Take your mind to a peaceful place

5. Stay in tune to your body's needs. Are you thirsty? Do you need a break? Are you hungry? If so then stop and tend to your body's needs.

Exercise does not need to cost money. Some people think that unless they are using heavy equipment or expensive equipment, then it is not true exercise. You do not need to buy any equipment.

Going for a walk in the park or in your neighborhood is an effective way to unleash any fear or anxiety. Fears are extinguished by overcoming what you are afraid of through slow and frequent intervention. There is nothing to be afraid of. You are one with nature when you are going for a walk in the neighborhood.

If part of your anxiety stems from being afraid to go outside, then know that you are not alone. Begin by taking baby steps. Start by going out with a friend or neighbor that you can trust. You do not have to disclose your fear to them, unless you want to.

Next, try to go out with your friend, but meet them at their door. You can call them and tell them that you are on your way. This may take you a couple of days to accomplish, but by not thinking about your fear, this allows you to recover.

Another option may be to only go out during daylight. This can give you the extra security that you may need to recover. As time progresses, you may want to try to go out at least one time at night just to see if you feel comfortable going outside in the night. However, always remember to be careful when going outside in the day or night. Use your street intelligence to guide you. If you need help with your street survival, then you may want to look into Official

Hood Survival Manual: Staying Safe in

the Streets, by Carmen S Gonzalez,

MS.Ed. and PO Block, AAS.

Take a deep breath and count to five

Materials:

None

Procedure:

1. Stop what you are doing and take a deep breath and inhale.
2. Exhale for 2 seconds.
3. Inhale and exhale for five counts. An alternative for taking two and calling someone in the morning can be to inhale and exhale. While

you are inhaling and exhaling you may want to focus on a positive thought. Some people like to focus on a chime or a bell to relieve their anxiety.

Inhaling and exhaling does not have to be done in an embarrassing manner. You do not need to cause a scene. It can be done in light breathes.

Love Cures All

Materials:

Trusted friend or relative

Some say that finding a trusted friend or

relative cures all anxiety. Some anxiety is

caused when one is afraid to trust in love.

Your love can be the love of life which is

the ultimate goal, however, what better way

to share the love of life than with another individual.

Try to spend at least 5 minutes of your day trying to share a bond or repair a bond with someone you care about. Tell them something that they probably never knew. Try to build a connection to them by sharing something that you both have in common.

Love cures all things. Love also cures anxiety. Some anxiety is caused because of lack of trust. When you learn to let go and trust another person, you gain a new and rejuvenated spirit.

<u>No matter how big or small…</u>

<u>Keep a journal</u>

Materials:

Journal

Pencil or Pen

Markers, glue, pictures (Optional)

No matter how big or small you think your thoughts may be these thoughts are the root of your cause for your anxiety. By keeping a journal, you are releasing all of your repressed thoughts and ideas.

When beginning a new journal, you may not know what to write. It is okay to take pictures and paste them in your journal. Pasting pictures in your journal are just as therapeutic. As time progresses, you will begin to see these pictures grow into words. This is the beginning of a new experience. Some people even love to draw pictures. This is okay as long as you feel the therapeutic satisfaction from the activity.

As time progresses, you may want to share your notebook with a trusted friend or a therapist. Your therapist will help you because now they have something to work with. Anxiety can only be healed when the person is aware that there is a problem.

Writing your thoughts down is a sign that you want to see growth. As time progresses your will notice that all of your repressed thoughts will be unveiled. You will grow into a better person because you see your own thoughts on paper. Many say seeing their thoughts on paper helps them because they feel a lot better, since they can see where these fears came from.

Always remember that if you do not know where your fears come from and if you feel like you are in danger or want to put someone else in danger that you should consult a professional. These are not signs of growth.

Music is the universal language of peace

Materials:

Music

Music is the universal language of peace. When you are feeling like you are overridden with anxiety, then a great strategy to use is to play calm relaxing music, preferably without any lyrics. The reason is because music without helps you focus on the rhythm of the music and not the words that caused the anxiety.

Music is something that cannot be taken away from you. Everyone has the ability to appreciate music. Music is a tool that has been used in many classrooms. Music helps children and adults by calming them down and not being as fearful or full of anxiety before an activity.

<u>Learn to say No</u>

Materials: Nothing

The ability to learn to say no is so important.

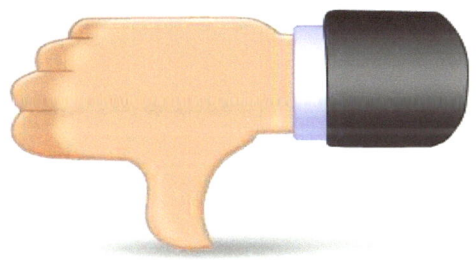

No is important because when you

learn to say no, you relieve yourself of the

stress that was caused when you continued to say yes to things that caused you pain.

Sometimes you may have to say no to even those you love, but at the end you will feel like you have less anxiety on your back.

Say no to illegal drugs and your anxiety symptoms will be minimized. This may mean that you have to cut off some of your friends. In the long run you will cut those expensive medical bills by more than half.

<u>Authors Note:</u>

Always remember to always consult a physician when you or someone you are about is in danger. Having anxiety is a serious medical condition that only a physician can diagnose. Do not attempt to self-diagnose yourself.